A SHARED GRANDMOTHER'S JOURNAL

An Interactive Treasure for You and Your Grandchild

MARIANNE WAGGONER DAY

ROCKRIDGE
PRESS

Interior and Cover Designer: Lindsey Dekker
Production Designer: Steve Solution
Art Producer: Janis Akerman
Editor: Adrienne Ingrum
Production Editor: Matt Burnett
Cover Illustration: SeamlessPatterns/Shutterstock.
Interior Photography: Images used under license from Shutterstock and istock; p. 36: Nadine Greeff Photography.

ISBN: Print 978-1-64611-024-7
R0

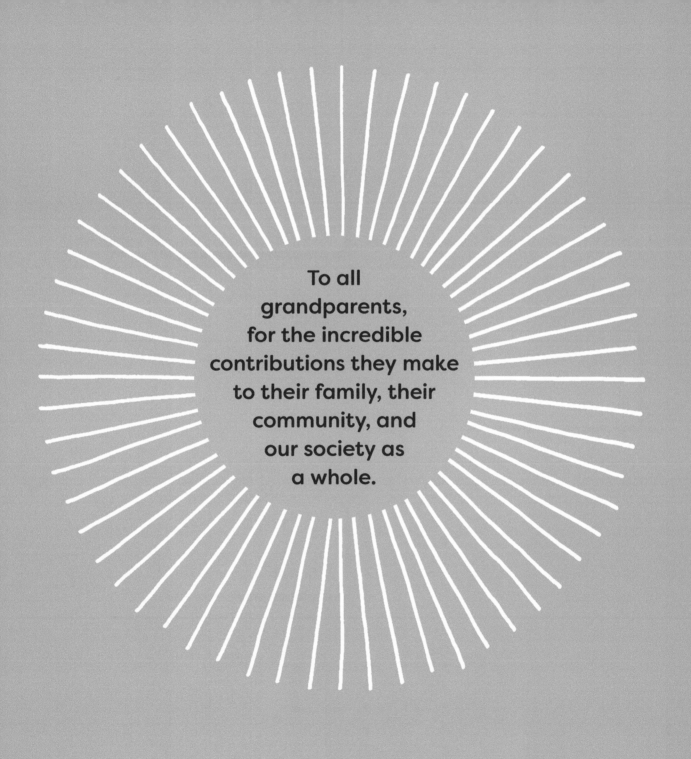

To all
grandparents,
for the incredible
contributions they make
to their family, their
community, and
our society as
a whole.

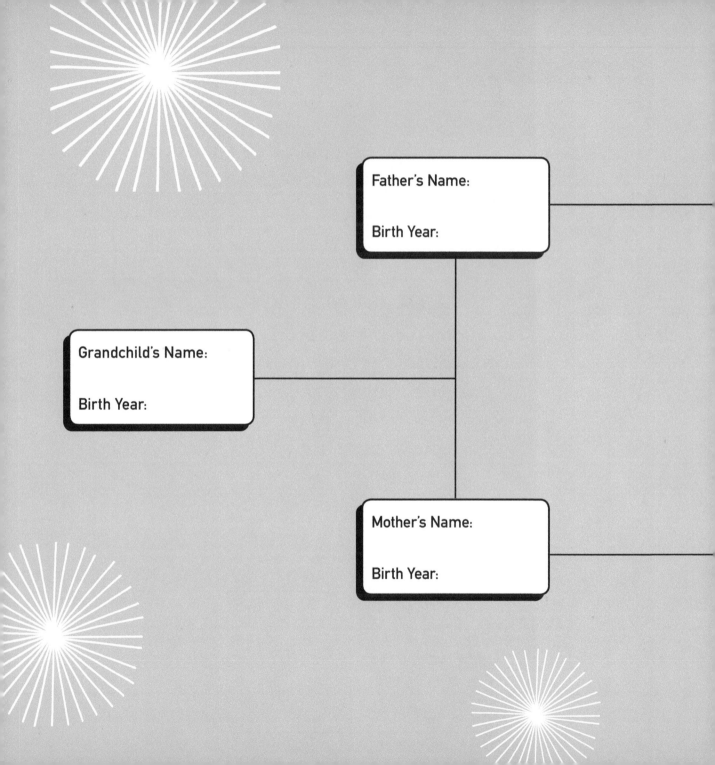

Father's Name:

Birth Year:

Grandchild's Name:

Birth Year:

Mother's Name:

Birth Year:

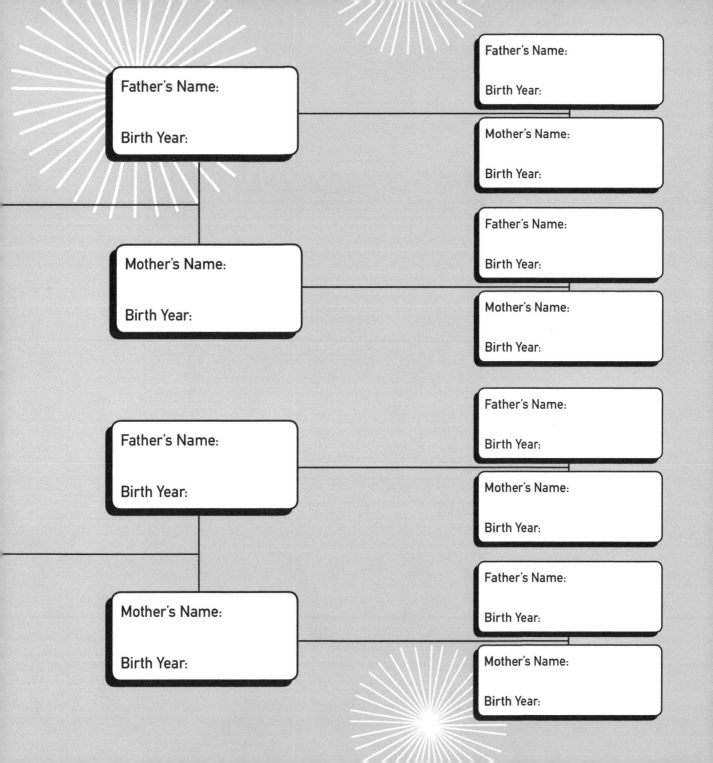

Father's Name:

Birth Year:

Mother's Name:

Birth Year:

Father's Name:

Birth Year:

Mother's Name:

Birth Year:

Father's Name:

Birth Year:

Mother's Name:

Birth Year:

Father's Name:

Birth Year:

Mother's Name:

Birth Year:

Father's Name:

Birth Year:

Mother's Name:

Birth Year:

Father's Name:

Birth Year:

Mother's Name:

Birth Year:

ABOUT *A SHARED GRANDMOTHER'S JOURNAL*

Grandmothers want to have meaningful relationships with their grandchildren. However, many of us are at a loss as to how to create lasting bonds when our current culture is at the mercy of social media, smartphones, computers, and frantic schedules. We can sometimes feel disconnected and distant, and we may not know how to bridge that distance, either emotionally or physically.

Well, help has arrived! *A Shared Grandmother's Journal* offers a wonderful way to engage with your grandchild to help build strong and enduring ties. It is a road map to creating a journal of knowledge and memories intended to cross the generational divide—to start conversations and improve mutual communication. Through these activities you will get to know each other by sharing stories, feelings, likes, and dislikes—even dreams, wishes, and hopes. Completing the journal together will draw out your recollections of the past, your thoughts about the present, and your visions for the future.

Open the journal to any page—there's no need to start at the beginning. Or browse through the book and choose a topic of interest to both of you. You and your grandchild can then follow the prompts and record your thoughts or feelings.

It's fun to do this together—maybe as you sip hot cocoa on a cold wintery day or as you nibble cookies while sitting on a park bench under a shade tree. And if geographic distance keeps you from having face-to-face contact, do the activities over FaceTime or Skype. Whenever or wherever you are "together," enrich your time by bringing along the journal and engaging in answering the prompts.

It's important to note that your grandchild's age doesn't matter; this is a joyful and meaningful project for any age. Just begin. And while you are learning about each other, don't be surprised if you learn more about yourself in the process. This exchange of wisdom unlocks memories and encourages you to revisit and consider your own experiences, traditions, and values.

This is a gift—one you will enjoy now, as you grow closer to your grandchild, and one you will cherish even more as years go by and you revisit your entries. And maybe the most important gift of all is the moment this journal can provide, when you look up from your work together and say, "Tell me more."

ABOUT GRANDMOTHER

DATE

NAME

MAIDEN NAME

NAME OF SPOUSE/PARTNER

BIRTHDATE

BIRTHPLACE

NAMES OF PARENTS

NAMES OF BROTHERS AND SISTERS

CULTURAL HERITAGE

    MATERNAL

    PATERNAL

MY GRANDCHILD CALLS ME

WHERE I GREW UP

PLACES I HAVE LIVED

SCHOOLS I HAVE ATTENDED

OCCUPATION(S)

RELIGIOUS AFFILIATION

THIS BOOK WILL BE A TREASURED KEEPSAKE FOR ME BECAUSE

I HOPE THIS BOOK WILL

ABOUT GRANDCHILD

DATE

NAME

BIRTHDATE

BIRTHPLACE

NAMES OF PARENTS

NAMES OF BROTHERS AND SISTERS

CULTURAL HERITAGE

    MATERNAL

    PATERNAL

MY GRANDMOTHER CALLS ME

WHERE I GREW UP

PLACES I HAVE LIVED

SCHOOLS I HAVE ATTENDED

RELIGIOUS AFFILIATION

THIS BOOK WILL BE A TREASURED KEEPSAKE FOR ME BECAUSE

I HOPE THIS BOOK WILL

GRANDMOTHER

The first memory of my childhood is

_____

_____

_____

_____

_____

GRANDCHILD

The first memory of my childhood is

_____

_____

_____

_____

_____

GRANDMOTHER

My favorite game or toy growing up was

and I liked it because

_____

_____

_____

_____

_____

GRANDCHILD

My favorite game or toy is

and I like it because

_____

_____

_____

_____

_____

GRANDMOTHER

I love the sound of

because it makes me feel

GRANDCHILD

I love the sound of

because it makes me feel

_____

_____

_____

_____

_____

_____

_____

_____

GRANDMOTHER

I laugh out loud when I hear or see

_____

_____

My grandchild is funniest when

_____

_____

GRANDCHILD

I laugh out loud when I hear or see

_____

_____

My grandmother is funniest when

_____

_____

GRANDMOTHER

On rainy days it's fun to

_____

_____

_____

_____

GRANDCHILD

On rainy days it's fun to

_____

_____

_____

_____

GRANDMOTHER

I am happiest when

because

_____

_____

_____

_____

_____

_____

_____

_____

_____

_____

GRANDCHILD

I am happiest when
_____

because
_____

_____

_____

_____

_____

_____

_____

_____

_____

_____

GRANDMOTHER

What I like to do most with my grandchild is

because it makes me feel

GRANDCHILD

What I like to do most with my grandmother is

_____

_____

because it makes me feel

_____

_____

_____

_____

_____

_____

_____

_____

_____

GRANDMOTHER

The qualities I look for in a best friend are

My friends would describe me as

GRANDCHILD

The qualities I look for in a best friend are

My friends would describe me as

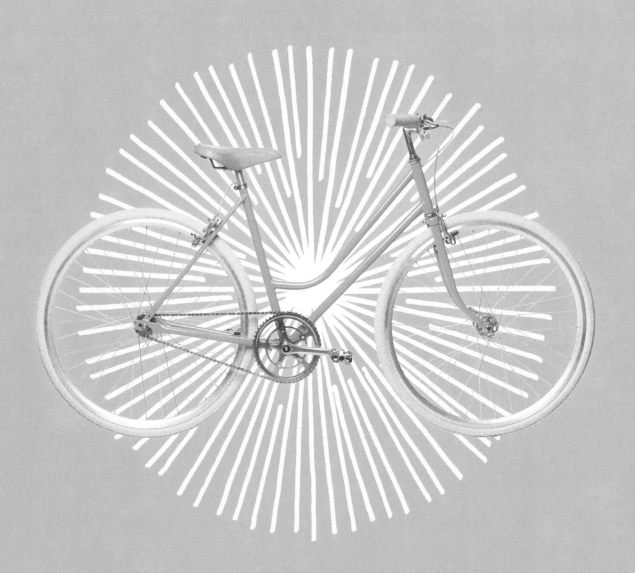

GRANDMOTHER

I would describe my childhood as

and this is why

GRANDCHILD

I would describe my childhood as

and this is why

GRANDMOTHER

When I was my grandchild's age, I would describe my typical day as

_____

_____

_____

_____

_____

_____

_____

_____

_____

GRANDCHILD

I would describe my typical day as

_____

_____

_____

_____

_____

_____

_____

_____

_____

_____

GRANDMOTHER

What I like best about myself is

because

GRANDCHILD

What I like best about myself is

because

GRANDMOTHER

My grandchild would be surprised to know that I

_____

_____

_____

_____

_____

_____

_____

_____

_____

_____

GRANDCHILD

My grandmother would be surprised to know that I

_____

_____

_____

_____

_____

_____

_____

_____

_____

_____

_____

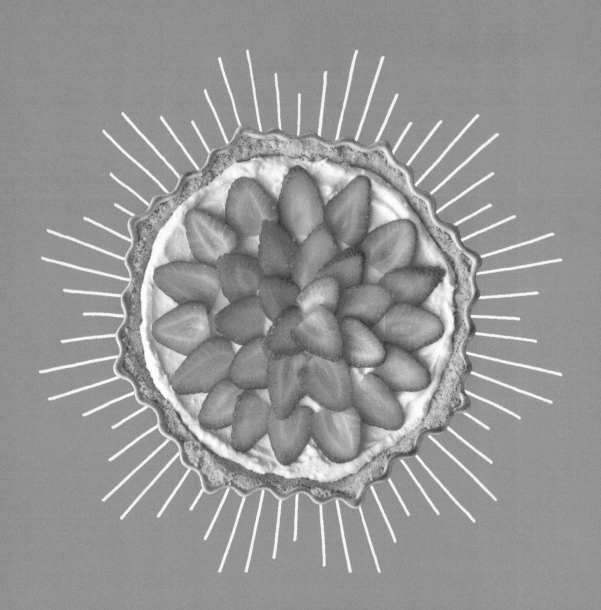

GRANDMOTHER

My favorite holiday tradition is

and I like it because

GRANDCHILD

My favorite holiday tradition is

and I like it because

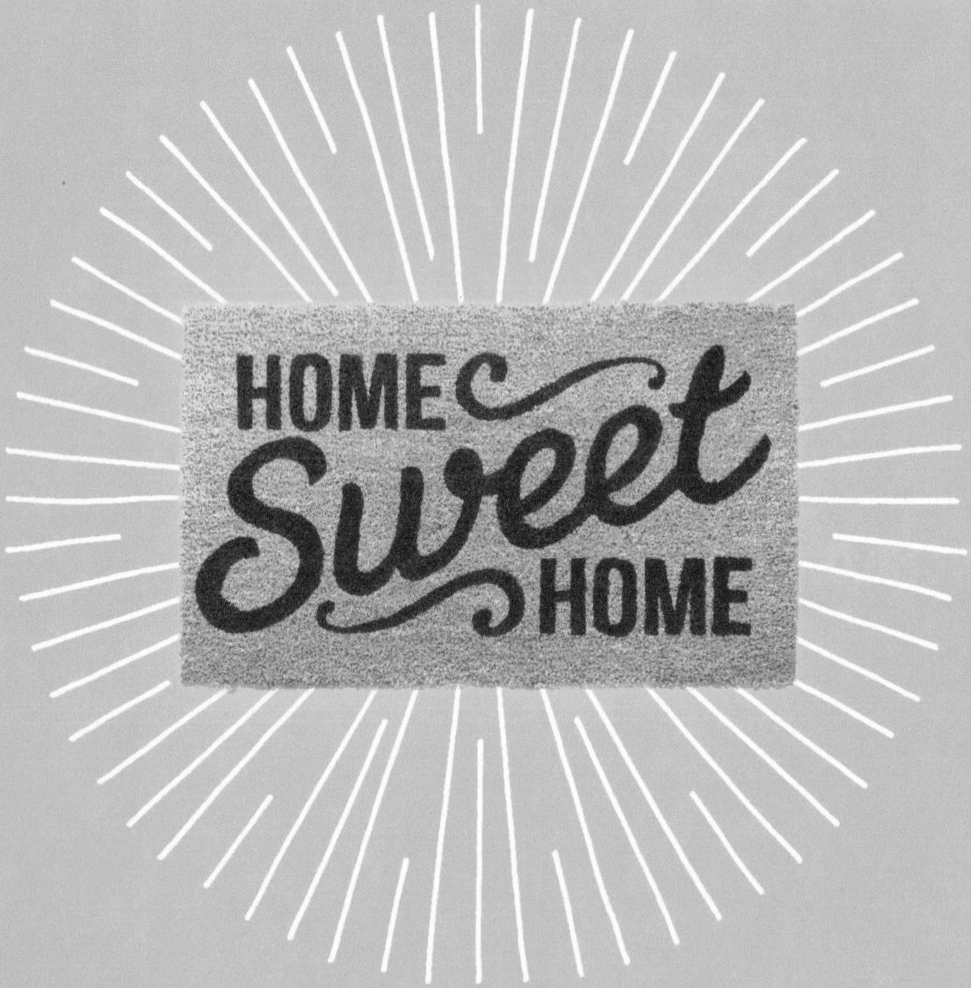
HOME
Sweet
HOME

GRANDMOTHER

My favorite family tradition is

because

GRANDCHILD

My favorite family tradition is

because

GRANDMOTHER

When I visit my grandchild, I always bring

because

GRANDCHILD

When I visit my grandmother, I always bring

because

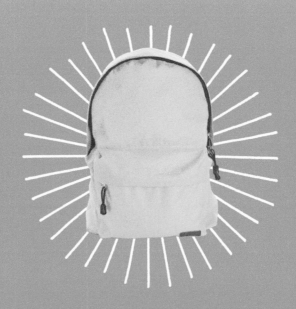

GRANDMOTHER

What scares me the most is

because

GRANDCHILD

What scares me the most is

because

GRANDMOTHER

My idea of an exciting adventure is

GRANDCHILD

My idea of an exciting adventure is

_____

_____

_____

_____

_____

_____

GRANDMOTHER

My hobbies include

_____

_____

_____

_____

_____

GRANDCHILD

My hobbies include

_____

_____

_____

_____

_____

GRANDMOTHER

What I like to do most with my friends is

_____

_____

_____

_____

GRANDCHILD

What I like to do most with my friends is

_____

_____

_____

_____

GRANDMOTHER

Before I go to sleep at night, I close my eyes and think about

_____

_____

_____

_____

_____

GRANDCHILD

Before I go to sleep at night, I close my eyes and think about

_____

_____

_____

_____

_____

GRANDMOTHER

I knew I had reached that magical age of being a grown-up when I could do these

three things:

_____

_____

_____

_____

GRANDCHILD

What does it mean to be a grown-up? I will know I have reached that magical age when I

can do these three things:

_____

_____

_____

_____

GRANDMOTHER

If I could change one thing about myself, it would be

because

GRANDCHILD

If I could change one thing about myself, it would be

because

GRANDMOTHER

At this moment in time, I think the world could use more

because

GRANDCHILD

At this moment in time, I think the world could use more
_____

because
_____

_____

_____

_____

_____

_____

_____

_____

_____

GRANDMOTHER

My favorite story about bravery, either true or make-believe, is

_____

_____

_____

_____

GRANDCHILD

My favorite story about bravery, either true or make-believe, is

_____

_____

_____

_____

GRANDMOTHER

The three things I most admire about my grandchild are

_____

_____

_____

_____

_____

_____

_____

_____

_____

_____

GRANDCHILD

The three things I most admire about my grandmother are

_____

_____

_____

_____

_____

_____

_____

_____

_____

_____

GRANDMOTHER

I know I should eat more

_____

but when no one is looking, I like to eat

_____

_____

_____

GRANDCHILD

I know I should eat more

_____

but when no one is looking, I like to eat

_____

_____

_____

GRANDMOTHER

I avoid

because it makes me feel

GRANDCHILD

I avoid

because it makes me feel

GRANDMOTHER

When I imagine the perfect day, it would be

_____

_____

_____

_____

_____

_____

_____

_____

_____

_____

GRANDCHILD

When I imagine the perfect day, it would be

_____

_____

_____

_____

_____

_____

_____

_____

_____

_____

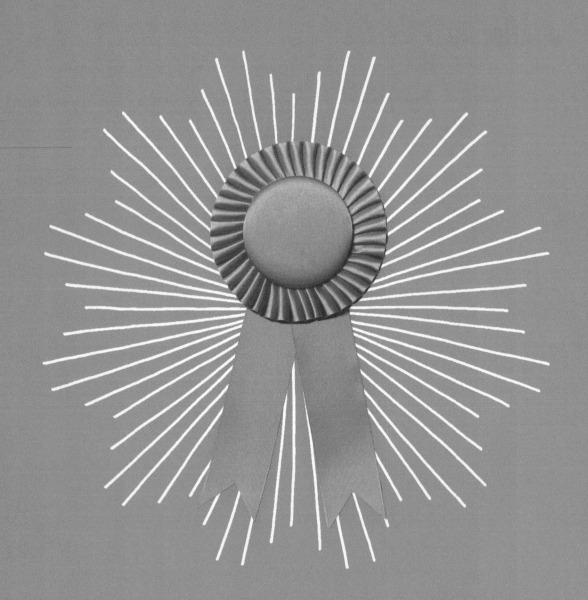

GRANDMOTHER

I remember being very proud of myself when I

_____

_____

_____

_____

GRANDCHILD

I remember being very proud of myself when I

_____

_____

_____

_____

GRANDMOTHER

It's fun to make a wish when I blow out the candles on my birthday cake.

One of my birthday wishes that came true was

One wish that never came true was

GRANDCHILD

It's fun to make a wish when I blow out the candles on my birthday cake.

One of my birthday wishes that came true was

One wish that never came true was

GRANDMOTHER

The greatest gift I ever received was

when

The best gift I have ever given to someone else was

and giving it made me feel

GRANDCHILD

The greatest gift I ever received was

when

The best gift I have ever given to someone else was

and giving it made me feel

GRANDMOTHER

If I could spend an afternoon talking with one of my ancestors, I would choose

and I would ask about

GRANDCHILD

If I could spend an afternoon talking with one of my ancestors, I would choose

and I would ask about

GRANDMOTHER

I liked the time I taught my grandchild to

_____

_____

If I could teach my grandchild one thing (skill or activity), it would be

because

_____

_____

GRANDCHILD

I liked the time my grandmother taught me to

_____

_____

If I could teach my grandmother one thing (skill or activity), it would be

because

_____

_____

GRANDMOTHER

The last time I danced was

and I was

GRANDCHILD

The last time I danced was

and I was

GRANDMOTHER

The most important lesson I have learned in life is

_____

and it is valuable to me because

_____

_____

_____

_____

_____

_____

_____

_____

GRANDCHILD

The most important lesson I have learned in life is

_____

_____

and it is valuable to me because

_____

_____

_____

_____

_____

_____

_____

_____

GRANDMOTHER

I like hearing about the time my grandchild

_____

_____

_____

_____

_____

The craziest thing I ever remember doing with my grandchild is

_____

_____

_____

_____

_____

GRANDCHILD

I like hearing about the time my grandmother

_____

_____

_____

_____

_____

The craziest thing I ever remember doing with my grandmother is

_____

_____

_____

_____

_____

GRANDMOTHER

A résumé is a brief statement of one's accomplishments and experience.

If I were writing my résumé, I'd say my greatest accomplishments so far are

_____

_____

_____

_____

_____

_____

_____

_____

_____

GRANDCHILD

A résumé is a brief statement of one's accomplishments and experience.

If I were writing my résumé, I'd say my greatest accomplishments so far are

_____

_____

_____

_____

_____

_____

_____

_____

_____

GRANDMOTHER

I remember my first job. I was _____ years old

and I worked at, or was, _____

What I liked about it was _____

_____

_____

_____

_____

GRANDCHILD

I hope to work at, or to be, _____

because _____

_____

_____

_____

GRANDMOTHER

My greatest strength is

_____

_____

_____

_____

GRANDCHILD

My greatest strength is

_____

_____

_____

_____

GRANDMOTHER

When I look at my grandchild, I'm reminded of

_____

_____

_____

_____

_____

GRANDCHILD

When I look at my grandmother, I'm reminded of

_____

_____

_____

_____

_____

GRANDMOTHER

I prefer to communicate by [talking, texting, writing emails or letters]

because

GRANDCHILD

I prefer to communicate by [talking, texting, writing emails or letters]

because

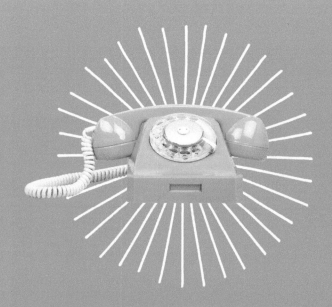

GRANDMOTHER

A legacy represents the contribution we make to the world. At this point in my life,

I think my legacy might be

GRANDCHILD

A legacy represents the contribution we make to the world. At this point in my life,

I think my legacy might be

GRANDMOTHER

My most difficult challenge so far in life has been

_____

_____

_____

_____

_____

_____

_____

_____

_____

GRANDCHILD

My most difficult challenge so far in life has been

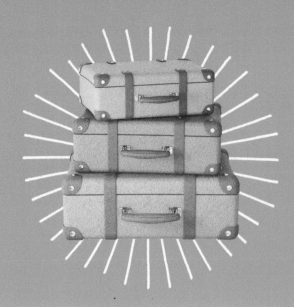

GRANDMOTHER

The farthest distance I have traveled is to

and I have visited these countries:

and I have visited these states:

GRANDCHILD

The farthest distance I have traveled is to

and I have visited these countries:

and I have visited these states:

GRANDMOTHER

What I like most about technology (computers, smartphones, etc.) is how I can

_____

_____

_____

_____

_____

_____

_____

_____

_____

_____

GRANDCHILD

What I like most about technology (computers, smartphones, etc.) is how I can

_____

_____

_____

_____

_____

_____

_____

_____

_____

_____

GRANDMOTHER

What makes me unique is

_____

_____

_____

_____

_____

GRANDCHILD

What makes me unique is

_____

_____

_____

_____

_____

GRANDMOTHER

Grandparents are different from parents. This is how being a grandmother is

different from being my grandchild's parent:

_____

_____

_____

_____

_____

_____

_____

_____

GRANDCHILD

Grandparents are different from parents. This is how my grandmother is

different from my parents:

_____

_____

_____

_____

_____

_____

_____

_____

_____

GRANDMOTHER

These are some ways someone can say, "I love you":

_____

_____

_____

_____

_____

GRANDCHILD

These are some ways someone can say, "I love you":

_____

_____

_____

_____

GRANDMOTHER

One of my favorite stories about your mom or dad growing up is

_____

_____

_____

_____

_____

_____

_____

_____

_____

_____

GRANDCHILD

One of my favorite stories about my mom or dad growing up is

_____

_____

_____

_____

_____

_____

_____

_____

_____

GRANDMOTHER

My favorite type of story or book is

_____

_____

_____

_____

_____

GRANDCHILD

My favorite type of story or book is

_____

_____

_____

_____

_____

GRANDMOTHER

I am lucky to know or to have

because

When I count my blessings, I always include

GRANDCHILD

I am lucky to know or to have
_____

because
_____

_____

_____

When I count my blessings, I always include
_____

_____

_____

GRANDMOTHER

This is what I think it takes to be happy:

_____

_____

_____

_____

_____

_____

_____

_____

_____

_____

GRANDCHILD

This is what I think it takes to be happy:

_____

_____

_____

_____

_____

_____

_____

_____

_____

GRANDMOTHER

I think of my grandchild when I hear the song

because
_____

_____

_____

_____

_____

GRANDCHILD

I think of my grandmother when I hear the song

because
_____

_____

_____

_____

_____

GRANDMOTHER

If I were a wild animal, I would be a(n)

because

GRANDCHILD

If I were a wild animal, I would be a(n)

because

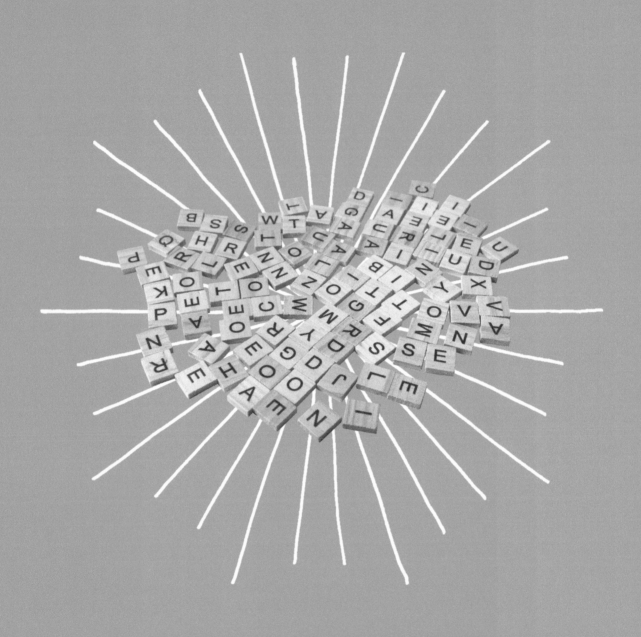

GRANDMOTHER

If I could have a different name, I would call myself

because it sounds more

GRANDCHILD

If I could have a different name, I would call myself

because it sounds more

GRANDMOTHER

If I could be a professional athlete or an Olympic champion, my sport would be

because

GRANDCHILD

If I could be a professional athlete or an Olympic champion, my sport would be

because

GRANDMOTHER

If I were a time traveler, I would like to travel back in time to

to see or meet

GRANDCHILD

If I were a time traveler, I would like to travel back in time to

to see or meet

GRANDMOTHER

If I could spend the day with a famous person, it would be

so I could learn about

GRANDCHILD

If I could spend the day with a famous person, it would be

so I could learn about

GRANDMOTHER

If I were the president of the United States for one day, I would

_____

_____

_____

_____

_____

GRANDCHILD

If I were the president of the United States for one day, I would

_____

_____

_____

_____

_____

GRANDMOTHER

If I could relive any day in my life—one that was especially fun or memorable—

it would be

because

_____

_____

_____

_____

_____

_____

_____

_____

_____

GRANDCHILD

If I could relive any day in my life—one that was especially fun or memorable—

it would be

because

_____

_____

_____

_____

_____

_____

_____

_____

_____

GRANDMOTHER

I love remembering the time I went to

with my grandchild because they showed me

_____

_____

_____

_____

GRANDCHILD

I love remembering the time I went to

with my grandmother because she showed me

_____

_____

_____

_____

GRANDMOTHER

If I am ever stranded on a desert island, the one thing I want to have with me is

because

GRANDCHILD

If I am ever stranded on a desert island, the one thing I want to have with me is

because

GRANDMOTHER

If I could be whatever age I wanted to be, I would choose to be

because

_____

_____

_____

_____

_____

GRANDCHILD

If I could be whatever age I wanted to be, I would choose to be

because

_____

_____

_____

_____

_____

GRANDMOTHER

Superheroes have extraordinary powers and use them for good. If I could have

any superpower, I would choose

and I would use it to

_____

_____

_____

_____

_____

_____

_____

_____

_____

GRANDCHILD

Superheroes have extraordinary powers and use them for good. If I could have

any superpower, I would choose

and I would use it to

_____

_____

_____

_____

_____

_____

_____

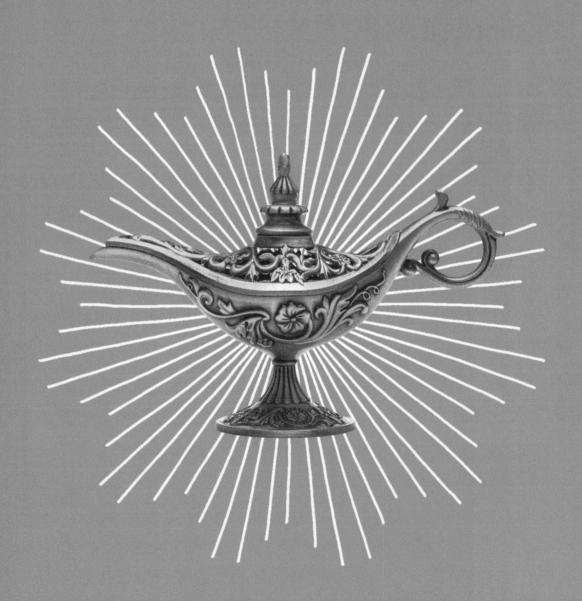

GRANDMOTHER

If I were walking on a desert trail and found a dirty old lamp (like Aladdin's lamp), I would pick

it up and wipe off the dirt. If a magical genie popped out and said they would grant me three

wishes, I would wish for

GRANDCHILD

If I were walking on a desert trail and found a dirty old lamp (like Aladdin's lamp), I would pick

it up and wipe off the dirt. If a magical genie popped out and said they would grant me three

wishes, I would wish for

GRANDMOTHER

I try to be a good grandmother by

_____

_____

_____

_____

_____

_____

_____

_____

_____

_____

_____

GRANDCHILD

I try to be a good grandchild by

_____

_____

_____

_____

_____

_____

_____

_____

_____

_____

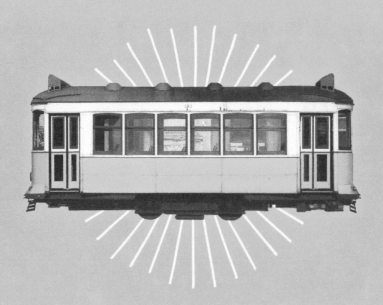

GRANDMOTHER

I hope to one day travel to

so I can see or experience

GRANDCHILD

I hope to one day travel to

so I can see or experience

GRANDMOTHER

If I were lucky enough to find a pot of gold at the end of a rainbow, this is what

I would do with it:

_____

_____

_____

_____

_____

GRANDCHILD

If I were lucky enough to find a pot of gold at the end of a rainbow, this is what

I would do with it:

_____

_____

_____

_____

_____

GRANDMOTHER

Goal setting is the process of identifying something you want to accomplish and

creating a plan to do it. Here are three goals I have for this year and why:

GRANDCHILD

Goal setting is the process of identifying something you want to accomplish and

creating a plan to do it. Here are three goals I have for this year and why:

_____

_____

_____

_____

_____

_____

_____

_____

_____

_____

GRANDMOTHER

My secret wish for myself was to be

_____

_____

_____

_____

_____

GRANDCHILD

My secret wish for myself is to be

_____

_____

_____

_____

_____

GRANDMOTHER

Fairy tales often end with "and they lived happily ever after." If I were to write my "happily ever after" ending, it would go like this:

_____

_____

_____

_____

_____

_____

_____

_____

_____

GRANDCHILD

Fairy tales often end with "and they lived happily ever after." If I were to write

my "happily ever after" ending, it would go like this:

_____

_____

_____

_____

_____

_____

_____

_____

GRANDMOTHER

I define my role as a grandmother as

_____

_____

_____

_____

The best thing about being a grandmother is

_____

_____

_____

_____

_____

GRANDCHILD

I define my role as a grandchild as

_____

_____

_____

_____

The best thing about being a grandchild is

_____

_____

_____

_____

_____

GRANDMOTHER

The most important thing I want you to know about me is

_____

_____

_____

_____

_____

GRANDCHILD

The most important thing I want you to know about me is

_____

_____

_____

_____

_____

GRANDMOTHER'S LIST OF FAVORITES

Color

Ice cream flavor

School subject

Outfit

Movie

Song

TV show

Outdoor game

Indoor game

Book

Musical instrument

Vegetable

Pet

Holiday

Fast-food restaurant

Pizza toppings

Cookie

Actor

Singer or musician

Planet

Amusement park

Dinosaur

Flower

Sea creature

Day of the week

Song

GRANDCHILD'S LIST OF FAVORITES

Color

Ice cream flavor

School subject

Outfit

Movie

Song

TV show

Outdoor game

Indoor game

Book

Musical instrument

Vegetable

Pet

Holiday

Fast-food restaurant

Pizza toppings

Cookie

Actor

Singer or musician

Planet

Amusement park

Dinosaur

Flower

Sea creature

Day of the week

Song

ABOUT THE AUTHOR

MARIANNE WAGGONER DAY is the author of *Camp Grandma: Next Generation Grandparenting—Beyond Babysitting*. She was a "typical" housewife and stay-at-home mother of the '60s and '70s—until her divorce necessitated "getting a job." She started her career in sales and was promoted to various management positions. Ultimately, she became president of retail services for CBRE, where she led the largest commercial retail real estate practice in the world. Day was the first woman to earn a Lifetime Achievement Award at the 100-year-old company. She was a frequent speaker and facilitated learning and training sessions.

Ten years ago she elected to step down from her corporate role while continuing to consult with former clients and coach high-performing business professionals. Now in retirement, she has come full circle—from having her picture in the *Wall Street Journal* to spending much of her day caring for her grandchildren. She started Camp Grandma for her four grandchildren and created lessons and activities from what she had learned in her work life. In this "corporate retreat" for children, she uses fun and engaging ways to teach valuable life skills, such as setting goals, being a team player, and speaking in front of a group. Along the way, she has observed the often-diminished and undervalued role of the grandparent in today's society. Grandparents are so much more than babysitters. Day wants to be the voice that elevates their "brand" and inspires ways to unlock even greater potential in this role.

Marianne resides with her husband in Southern California, where she is often asked to speak on the topic of grandparenting. She would love to hear from you. You can reach Marianne via:

Email: marianne@campgrandma.com

Facebook: facebook.com/mariannewaggonerday

LinkedIn: linkedin.com/in/marianne-waggoner-day-81687b162/